STOLEN RAINBOW

The Great Unmasking

By Martin Mawyer

Published by PRB Publishing.

Printed in the United States of America.

Cover Design:
Michael Mawyer

Editorial Consultant:
Alec Rooney

Interior Design & Layout:
Patti A. Pierucci

God's rainbow. We love to gaze upon it, photograph it, simply sit back and be awed by it on those rare occasions when it graces our skyline. It is a vast wonder that spans every color. The Bible calls it nothing less than a symbol of God's love for humanity.

Except that now it's hard to hear the word "rainbow" without a twinge of unease and distaste. It has acquired a new meaning. A twisted meaning.

It now means: *Gay Pride.*

Just as "rainbow" once referred to something natural and beautiful, the word "gay" used to mean lighthearted, happy, irrepressibly cheerful. But not anymore. Now it means: sexually attracted to your own gender.

What about the word "pride?" It, too, has a new meaning. A word that once described a feeling of accomplishment and self-worth has now been hijacked by homosexuals to mean anyone who is outspoken ... about being homosexual.

The twisting of accepted symbols is a hallmark of gay rights activism. Especially of positive symbols. And e specially symbols of godly things.

Gay activists will tell you that the different colors in the rainbow flag represent harmony, co-existence, and being part of a diverse sexual tapestry. Why are we, as Christians, not feeling that harmony?

The natural inclination is to turn our heads, cover our eyes, stick our fingers in our ears, zip our lips and not talk about it. But as much as we may want to stamp this subject out of our heads, we can't escape it.

It's everywhere.

It is in news articles, awards ceremonies, school classrooms, libraries, pageants, sporting events, product labels and even toys. It's trumpeted on cereal boxes, in television shows and commercials, in comic books, on flagpoles. You hear about it in songs, see it on buses, police cars and fire engines, and are even reminded of it by dog collars and ID tags.

A gay-themed baby carriage? It's available. Gay-themed baby clothes? Sure, they are being sold as well. Gay-themed Jesus shirts, jackets or caps? It's nearly incomprehensible, but they're just a click away on the Internet.

And the crowning, colorful, co-opted symbol that has come to represent a preference for sex with your own gender? God's rainbow.

The rainbow, with all its color and mystery, has come to represent merely the "pride" of being gay, lesbian, bisexual, transgender or queer. Or, in the ever-lengthening shorthand abbreviation, "LGBTQ."

Only this "inclusivity" club is surprisingly non-inclusive. Notice that there's no H, for heterosexuality. Heterosexuals are excluded. But we know better than to complain, right?

Looking for the End of the Rainbow

Not surprisingly, the hijacking of our beautiful, important rainbow began in a hotbed of gay culture, New York City's Greenwich Village. The exact place was called the Stonewall Inn.

The original Stonewall Inn, which operated between 1967 and 1969, was located on Christopher Street, between West 4th Street and Waverly Place. It no longer exists.

At its founding, the Stonewall Inn was a mafia-controlled, high-priced bar that sold watered-down whiskey to a homosexual clientele and under-aged kids. With no license to sell liquor, the establishment was the target of frequent police raids.

Greenwich Village was the place to be if you were gay or lesbian or enjoyed dressing in drag. It was also the place to be if you enjoyed having gay sex in public.

Ed Koch, a Democratic leader in the Greenwich Village area, would say there were gays "who would have sex on the streets. And the Village has a lot of people with children, and they were offended."

On June 28th, 1969, New York police raided the Stonewall, as they often did, looking for illegal alcohol and the money it brought in. The police had no intention of arresting any of the cross-dressing homosexuals. Deputy Inspector Seymour Pine, the officer in charge, would say the raid's only purpose was confiscating illegal alcohol and the cash made from those contraband sales.

The Stonewall Inn in Greenwich Village, NY, where the gay pride movement in America began.* (Flickr photo by Victoria Pickering)

2

In previous raids the patrons — mainly transvestites — would exit the tavern doors and scurry back home.

On that particular night, in a raid at 1 a.m., things took a different and violent turn.

The homosexual community felt these shakedowns weren't directed at the mafia. They felt they were the targets — particularly those who dressed in drag. At the time, the law in New York City required a person to wear at least three articles of clothing specific to that person's gender.

> **❛ Our goal was to hurt those police. I wanted to kill those cops for the anger I had in me.**

Rather than go home, the mostly transvestite patrons staged a pushback that would turn into a fiery, violent riot.

They called police "pigs" and started throwing pennies at them while shouting "coppers." They rocked police cars, trying to flip them over, and tried touching the officers sexually.

Fearing for their lives, the police sought safety inside the bar. The crowd grew larger by the minute. People stood on police cars and trash cans, screaming and yelling. Objects were thrown against the plywood covering the restaurant windows. Someone lit a fire. Then firebombs were thrown into the bar as the police pushed to keep the doors closed. The police had to douse the flames with nothing but small water hoses and a fire extinguisher. Three or four protesters ripped a parking meter from the pavement and the drag queens used it as a battering ram on the front doors.

Deputy Inspector Pine would say, "It was terrifying. It was as bad as any situation that I had met during my entire time in the Army."

One protester said, "Our goal was to hurt those police. I wanted to kill those cops for the anger I had in me."

For some unexplained reason police radios were disabled, preventing officers from calling for backup.

With six officers barricaded inside the bar and several thousand agitators now gathered outside, panic began to set in.

Then, to the relief of the trapped policemen, sirens wailed in the distance. Law enforcement reserves came by the busload with tactical equipment. They formed a phalanx and marched down Christopher Street, pushing against the crowd, hoping shields and batons would be enough to disperse the angry mob.

3

It didn't work. The crowd pushed back and circled the Stonewall Inn. They came in from behind, using side streets, and gathered courage as they saw their own reinforcements coming from every direction. The fiery violence went on for hours. Police officers were beaten and some were taken to the hospital.

The police were equally unyielding. They charged back and began hitting heads with clubs. More police arrived and the fighting became fiercer.

Windows were broken. Garbage cans were set on fire and thrown at police. Police cars were flipped and had their tires slashed. So it went on, all night long, until the rioters tired and went home.

The events at the Stonewall Inn would inspire the first gay pride parade in the United States. On June 28, 1970, a march was led from Greenwich Village to the Sheep Meadow in Central Park.

Gay historian Linda Hirshman would write in her book, *Victory: The Triumphant Gay Revolution,* "the attitude of the homosexual community was to either kill the police or be treated fairly."

Building up the Movement

Despite this fiery and violent start in 1969, the homosexual community as a movement struggled to find a public voice, a unified agenda and an organizational structure. They were missing something else, as well: significant support from non-homosexuals.

In those early days, the movement's most successful achievements were electing a few gay candidates to public office. Most notable was gay-rights activist Harvey Milk.

Milk became a San Francisco supervisor in 1977. In 1978, however, he was assassinated, along with the city's mayor, George Moscone. The assassin was former San Francisco Supervisor Dan White. The killings had nothing to do with Milk's homosexuality, but rather stemmed from a political dispute between Dan White and the San Francisco mayor.

Poster of gay rights icon Harvey Milk at pride parade.* (Flickr photo)

Dan White had recently resigned his post as a supervisor, but changed his mind shortly afterward. He wanted

4

to retake his seat. The mayor initially agreed but then changed his mind after Harvey Milk vigorously opposed the reappointment.

On November 26, White arrived at City Hall and climbed through a first-floor window carrying a .38 caliber revolver and 10 rounds of ammunition. His mission was to shoot and kill everyone who had opposed his reappointment.

White shot Moscone twice in the head before walking across the city building to find Milk in his office. He reloaded his gun and shot Milk five times, killing him.

White then fled the building and turned himself in at San Francisco's Northern Police Station, where he had once served as an officer.

The gay community saw an opportunity. They began promoting the myth that Harvey Milk was assassinated for his homosexuality. In fact, Milk, as a martyr for gay rights, was a complete fabrication.

Dan White, the killer, was far from being anti-homosexual. White had recently opposed a California ballot initiative that would have banned gays and lesbians from working in public schools.

Nevertheless, the homosexual movement lionized Milk as their first so-called martyr.

That wasn't all that the gay community needed in June 1978, nearly ten years after the Stonewall Inn riots. They also needed a banner to rally their community into political activism.

That assignment went to one of San Francisco's most flamboyant gay artists, Gilbert Baker.

A Bitter, Angry Artist

Gilbert Baker was born in Chanute, Kansas, in 1951 and grew up in the small town of Parsons, where his grandmother owned a women's clothing store. His father was a judge. His mother was a teacher. He joined the Army in 1970 and served as a medic in the city of San Francisco.

He was a gifted artist and tailor. He had also been a friend of the homosexual San Francisco supervisor, Harvey Milk. Baker would arrive in the Golden City only months after Milk's murder.

Baker was a known gay rights activist. He was a proponent of legalized marijuana and, more controversially, would soon be a member of a homosexual drag queen group known for mocking Christians, the Sisters of Perpetual Indulgence.

In 1978, San Francisco organizers of the Gay Freedom Day Parade felt the homosexual community needed a flag to unify the

Gay rights activist and artist Gilbert Baker as "Pink Jesus" in a gay pride parade. (From a screenshot from "Pink Jesus, A Christmas Story," YouTube)

movement and display its Pride (with a capital P). It would need to be a catchy symbol that could inspire non-gay people to sympathize with their cause.

Gilbert Baker, a man who had enough hatred for Christianity to join the Sisters of Perpetual Indulgence, got the job.

On June 25, 1978, Baker debuted his gay rainbow flag in a grand unfurling at the United Nations Plaza in front of 250,000 spectators.

The colors that had previously symbolized God's rainbow and His love for mankind were now officially the logo of special rights for gays and lesbians.

It caught on.

In 1970, a mere 30 people attended San Francisco's Gay Freedom Day Parade. By 2019, the number had grown to a remarkable 1.8 million attendees.

In Washington, D.C., the first-ever homosexual march on the nation's capital in 1979 drew between 75,000 and 125,000 gay, lesbian, transgender and other homosexual rights sympathizers.

That was also the year the Sisters of Perpetual Indulgence got together, providing rainbow flag designer Gilbert Baker with an outlet for his hostility toward Christians.

Besides mocking Christianity, with most of its venom directed at the Catholic Church, the Sisters of Perpetual Indulgence promoted gender-bending, the attempt to destroy rigid gender roles and defiance of sex-role stereotypes.

Composed chiefly of men sporting facial hair, group members dress creepily in nuns' habits and clown makeup. Members also adopt absurd and obscene names meant to shock and offend Christians.

In 1999 the Sisters of Perpetual Indulgence launched an annual festival in San Francisco called the "Hunky Jesus" contest, held at Golden Gate Park during Easter celebrations.

Organizers billed the event as being "easily considered blasphemy and insulting to Christians." They didn't disappoint.

But mocking Christ's resurrection was nothing new to gay pride rainbow designer Gilbert Baker. As far back as 1990, Baker took to the streets as a pink homosexual Jesus, off to be crucified because he was a homosexual.

> ❝ I'm all about working every last nerve of the Church. So I decided we should ... have gay Jesus, right? Jesus is gay, everybody thought that anyway.

Baker later explained that his pink Jesus theatrics were a show of support for the equally controversial shock-artist Andres Serrano. In 1987, Serrano used taxpayer money from the National Endowment for the Arts to create a blasphemous photo called *Piss Christ*.

Piss Christ depicted a miniature plastic crucifix submerged in a glass jar of the artist's urine. Baker would call *Piss Christ* "a very beautiful photograph."

In a recorded interview, Gilbert Baker said he was "all about working every last nerve of the church":

> *"I'm a Sister of Perpetual Indulgence. I'm all about working every last nerve of the Church. So I decided we should not only have Piss Christ, but we should have gay Jesus, right? Jesus is gay, everybody thought that anyway, so Pink Jesus. And I was already good in heels and I looked like Jesus ... It definitely added to my very questionable reputation ... A couple of weeks later, my sister calls and she says, 'Oh, I saw your picture.' I said, 'Oh, really? What are you talking about?' She said, 'Oh, yeah. I was with mom and we saw it in the Enquirer at the grocery store.' And I could just imagine my poor mother."*

Whatever regrets Baker might have had for offending his poor mother, he never showed any regrets for insulting Christian believers around the world before his death in 2017.

By his own words, Gilbert Baker was that man determined to work every last nerve of the Church. First, he proposed that Jesus Christ was a homosexual, and later he claimed Christ shed His blood to defend gay sex. Finally, he would seal his well-documented hatred for the Christian religion by praising the "beauty" of a photograph of Christ and His Cross submerged in a jar of urine.

The gay rainbow flag claims to be a symbol of gay pride, but it's really a symbol of hatred — hatred of Christians — designed by an artist whose goal was to hurt and offend.

From Parades to AIDS

Turning God's truths upside down would soon come to define the militant wing of the homosexual movement. Devout Christians believed the Bible had been turned on its head with such homosexual claims as God ordaining same-sex marriages. Or that parents, rather than God and biology, can determine a child's gender. Or that people have the option of changing their own God-given sex. Or that men have wombs that can nurture a child. Or that Christ was a homosexual who was crucified for it. Or that God created the rainbow to celebrate the gay lifestyle rather than His love for and covenant with mankind.

The power and importance of flags as symbols of political, social or religious causes cannot be underestimated. A flag is a beacon and a magnet for the like-minded. It is a rallying point and symbol of purpose that unites people behind a cause, crusade or philosophy. Flags have an almost mystical power to instill courage, sacrifice and determination. A well-designed flag can be an extremely powerful thing.

But what really is a flag? Physically, it's a piece of fabric with colors, designs and sometimes words. So how does such a simple thing come to be seen as almost holy, or in some cases, cursed, the very embodiment of darkness and evil?

Nazi Germany provides an example.

The swastika was originally a sign of well-being. Adolf Hitler's desire was for the German people to think they were they were fighting for the well-being of the nation, not for world domination, racial purity or the elimination of the Jewish people.

Hitler understood the power of imagery, and said as much. The leader of the Nazi party would say: "An effective insignia can, in hundreds of thousands of cases, give the first impetus towards interest in a movement."

Hitler, more than any single human being, would teach the world horrible lessons. The flag itself never truly defines a movement. Its creator does.

In the case of the gay-themed rainbow flag, the creator was a man obsessed by his hatred toward Christ's church, who marched in parades to disparage Christianity and who took pleasure in an artist's depiction of Christ and His cross in a jar of human urine.

Yet despite Gilbert Baker's mockery and meanness, the rainbow

"Piss Christ" by Andres Serrano consisted of a crucifix submerged in a jar of the artist's own urine.

flag flew over an increasingly global phenomenon.

Whereas previous gay parades enjoyed, at most, crowds in the hundreds, by 1980 those same celebrations — united and energized under the rainbow flag — would swell into the thousands and tens of thousands.

Those enthusiastic rallies would be short-lived, however.

The fire sparked by that rainbow flag would be quickly doused in 1981 with the sudden and mysterious outbreak of a disease known by four capital letters: AIDS.

AIDS, or acquired immune deficiency syndrome, is caused by HIV, the human immunodeficiency virus. The disease attacks the body's immune system, leaving it nearly defenseless against common infections. Without treatment, the life expectancy of people who get the disease is around ten years.

Though humans can contract the disease through blood transfusions and contaminated hypodermic needles, AIDS is primarily transmitted through homosexual sex, meaning anal sex. Today it can be controlled, but it still has no real cure.

By the early 1980s AIDS had come to be known as the "gay cancer," and it was frequently ridiculed as the "booty flu" and the "immaculate injection."

By the end of 1986, more than 45,000 Americans would be dead of AIDS-related illnesses.

AIDS hysteria was a setback of biblical proportions for the homosexual movement during the 1980s. In many ways, those setbacks are

9

still being felt today.

Heightening the hysteria were high-profile deaths from AIDS.

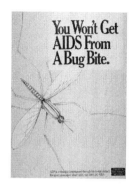

Heartthrob actor Rock Hudson died in 1985 from AIDS. The flamboyant pianist Liberace died of AIDS in 1987. Anthony Perkins, who played Norman Bates in Alfred Hitchcock's 1960 horror classic film *Psycho,* was diagnosed with AIDS in the 1980s and died from the infection in 1992. Amanda Blake, who played Miss Kitty on the 1960s TV show *Gunsmoke,* caught AIDS from her bisexual husband, Mark Spaeth. The famous screen actress would die from AIDS in 1989.

One of the most notable deaths would be that of Freddie Mercury of the rock supergroup Queen. The operatic singer and songwriter was diagnosed with AIDS in 1987 and would die at age 45 from the disease in 1991.

These celebrity deaths struck fear into the hearts of Americans. They had plenty of questions: Who was vulnerable? How contagious was the virus? Who should be avoided? How do you know if someone is carrying the AIDS virus?

Public reaction was understandably harsh, panicky and impulsive. Due to public fear of catching the disease, which at the time meant certain death, the Centers for Disease Control began running public service announcements to put a worried nation at ease. Assurances that people couldn't catch AIDS from swimming in pools, eating at restaurants, playing hide-and-seek or from a bug bite were meant to calm a deeply worried public.

One thing the CDC couldn't deny, however, was that AIDS was transmissible through blood transfusions. This was a serious cause of concern to the 4.5 million Americans who annually re-

The CDC's "America's Response To Aids" campaign was in response to public fear of the disease in the early years of the AIDS epidemic.

ceive them.

In 1985, the U.S. Food and Drug Administration banned gay men from donating blood. Around the same time, the CDC would have to admit that AIDS was not a contagious disease in the traditional sense. AIDS, the CDC would clarify, was almost exclusively contracted through sex acts involving blood, such as anal sex, or through the sharing of hypodermic needles among infected drug users.

Gay bathhouses across the United States began to close. Christian leaders used the heightened alarm to demand an end to the advancement of special rights for homosexuals. The disease would elevate such conservative and religious figures as entertainer Anita Bryant, Senator Jesse Helms and the Rev. Jerry Falwell to household names.

Well-known liberal minister Rev. William Sloane Coffin said he counseled many people living with AIDS who "felt that this was in some way God's punishment." He assured them that it was not, and told them being gay was not a sin.

God's punishment or not, by the end of the 1980s more than 100,000 Americans had been diagnosed with AIDs, the vast majority of them homosexuals. Whether they had the disease or not, homosexuals faced an angry public that held them directly responsible.

Gay men lost their jobs. Some were evicted from apartment complexes. Funeral home directors reportedly refused to accept the bodies of dead AIDS patients. Hospitals were accused of turning away AIDS patients who were dying. Some homosexuals became hooked on drugs to alleviate the pain of seeing friends dying all around them. Other gays would go back into the closet, fearful of the social consequences of coming out.

"No one is safe from AIDS," blared *LIFE* magazine in July 1985. By 1993, Health and Human Services Secretary Donna Shalala had heightened that hysteria by telling Congress that AIDS could lead to "nobody left."

Such hysteria fueled by *LIFE*, Secretary Shalala and others would prove to be unscientific and disingenuous.

As an overwhelming majority of Americans would soon learn, they were never in any real danger of contracting HIV or the AIDS virus. Nevertheless, by 1990 AIDS had become America's first politicized virus, pushed as a disease that threatened to wipe out the entire world.

21st century Americans are now much more accustomed to government agencies, political leaders and the media politicizing a disease. That was not the case in the early 1990s. Several decades ago, it would have been unthinkable.

Looking back, there's no question that the statement from the secretary of Health and Human Services that AIDS was likely to kill off all Americans — leaving literally no survivors — was a political and not a medical statement. But why? What was the purpose?

The over-the-top statement would serve two purposes: First, to justify dishing out tax-payer money to the homosexual community; second, to garner public sympathy for gays and lesbians.

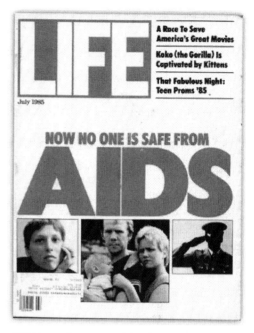

LIFE Magazine cover, July 1985

In Your Face and ACTing UP

The AIDS epidemic helped transition the homosexual community from a financially strapped political advocacy group to a well-funded civil rights group. The politicization of the disease started a stream of government aid pouring into the movement and a dramatic surge of support from sympathetic media. The gay community was now able to reimagine itself as a downtrodden minority group, oppressed by both man and disease.

By the mid-1990s, the gay rights movement was beginning to flex its muscle.

Rather than focusing solely on its struggle to legalize homosexual sex, the well-financed gay community was now drawing upon worldwide human sympathy that would answer its call for acceptance, tolerance and inclusion.

They succeeded. AIDS, though it took a physical toll on their health and numbers, gave them unimagined political clout. Their mantra was no longer just to keep government authority out of their bedrooms, but for governments to concede they were an actual minority in need of special protections, benefits, rights and privileges.

They used the plight of AIDS as a springboard to win some of the most astounding, far-reaching and ground-breaking special treatment ever achieved in American history, and would do it in record time.

Emboldened by both cash and sympathy, the movement relied less on peaceful marches and parades and more on "in your face" demonstrations to build on that success.

No group was better at taking to the streets with brash, strident demands than ACT-UP (AIDS Coalition to Unleash Power), and its offshoot sister organization Queer Nation, whose catchy slogan was, "We're here, We're Queer, Get used to it."

ACT-UP was founded in 1987 by the controversial and self-proclaimed "angriest gay man in the world," the late playwright and author Larry Kramer. Kramer said he was a proud, gay "loudmouth," and he enjoyed gutting his opponents publicly. He once accused the mayor of New York City, Ed Koch, of being a closeted homosexual, without any evidence. Kramer made other jaw-dropping accusations, such as that George Washington and Alexander Hamilton were secretly gay lovers, and that President Lincoln was assassinated over a lover's quarrel with John Wilkes Booth.

ACT-UP members under Larry Kramer's leadership were rowdy, purposely obnoxious and shameless by design. Wherever they went, they chanted and screamed through bullhorns, blocked cars on the streets with their bodies, and chained themselves to doors. In 1988, more than 100 ACT-UP protesters were arrested during a rally called Operation Wall Street.

They would storm offices of elected officials and throw fake blood over employee workstations. Then, before the police could arrive, they would lock themselves to politicians' desks. Even hospitals became targets of ACT-UP's theatrical disruptions. Members would pile into emergency room lobbies and stage mass "die-ins" and "kiss-ins."

In 1991, ACT-UP members traveled to the residence of late North Carolina Senator Jesse Helms in Arlington, Virginia. They draped the entire house of this outspoken critic of special rights for homosexuals in a giant condom.

In December 1991, ACT UP's Seattle chapter distributed more than 500 "safer-sex" packets outside Seattle high schools. The packets contained an explicit four-letter word to describe safe sex and included drawings of two men performing oral sex.

The *Seattle Times* would say, "ACT-UP Needs Its Filthy Mouth Washed Out." (Today, the liberal *Seattle Times* would probably praise them for their daunting courage to offend and agitate.)

ACT-UP would also distribute rubber gloves, lubricants and condoms to Seattle students.

It did not go unnoticed that ACT-UP's school-aged condom distribution campaign was, in part, intended as a direct slap against the Catholic Church. The Catholic Church had maintained that condoms were unlikely to prevent the spread of HIV or AIDs.

In 1989, a former producer for ABC's *Good Morning America*, Ann Northrop, told an ACT-UP gathering in New York that it was time to destroy the Catholic Church. She even accused its bishops of being murderers for objecting to prophylactic use.

ACT-UP quickly responded to Northrop's call for violence and launched a campaign called "Stop the Church." On Sunday, December 10, 1989, ACT-UP protesters stormed Manhattan's St. Patrick's Cathedral to shut it down.

While police prevented some protesters from entering, more than 100 gay activists — deceptively dressed in conservative clothing — made their way to the pews. They waited for an opportune moment to wreak havoc on the morning Mass.

The protest began with some ACT-UP members approaching the central aisle and throwing themselves on the floor, acting dead from the AIDS virus. But when this drama proved unimpressive to many churchgoers, ACT-UP member Michael Petrelis stood on a pew, blew a whistle and began shouting, "You're killing us!"

Not every ACT-UP member supported the theatrical extremism now shaping the movement. Some wanted the militancy contained, if not abandoned altogether. Many feared such visual spectacles as mass die-ins, the storming of office buildings, phony severed heads mounted on pikes, and obscenities shouted in front of small children, among other activities, would outrage pharmaceutical companies, which were beginning to offer jobs to homosexuals as consultants. Others, however, wanted the group to expand its aggressive tactics and escalate its public confrontations.

The internal divisions threatened to tear the organization apart.

Dismissing the concerns of moderate members, the leadership of ACT-UP stood behind their bare-knuckle theatrics, believing their rude, combative and obscenity-laced behavior was vital to their mission. As a result, the media elevated them to the dominant voice of the gay rights movement until the mid-1990s.

Their noise, disruptions and criminal acts not only got the attention of lawmakers but would eventually knock down doors of key government agencies — agencies that would later become critical for the advancement of their gay rights agenda.

The Clinton Effect

The 1992 election of Bill Clinton to the presidency launched the homosexual community as a political juggernaut. Clinton created the nation's first "AIDS Czar" and opened up other powerful federal posts to homosexual-rights sympathizers, such as Health and Human Services Secretary Donna Shalala.

"Unless with every bit of energy we have we are prepared to say that any American dying, no matter what their color, sex or sexual orientation, is a sister and brother of each one of us, there will not be much of America left and you have my commitment that we will not only make this a priority but it will be central in our minds as we move forward ahead over the next few years." (Secretary Donna Shalala)

Under the Clinton Administration, dire warnings about AIDS having the potential to kill all Americans would help introduce and spread homosexual sex education classes into public schools.

President Clinton increased federal spending on HIV and AIDS treatment and prevention by 73 percent during his eight years

Former President Bill Clinton created the first AIDS "czar."

in office, a funding total that reached $4.87 billion under his administration. His successors would follow with even more generous grants. By 2015, the total global spending on HIV research, treatment and prevention topped half a trillion dollars.

Although it is impossible to know how much of that money trickled down to gay rights activist groups, it is well-established that the homosexual movement — which existed in poverty in the 1980s and early '90s — would soon become one of the best-funded political powerhouses of the 21st century.

The money poured into the gay movement not only from federal, state and city grants, but from wealthy philanthropic groups like the Ford Foundation, the Gill Foundation and the Arcus Foundation.

The Arcus Foundation alone gave more than $58.4 million to pro-LGBTQ programs and causes between 2007 and 2010.

With money in the bank, it was time for the radical homosexual community to go public with their ever-escalating demands for special rights, benefits and programs. Starting in the mid-1990s and for the next 25 years, those demands were loud and clear.

The gay community wanted an end to laws that criminalized homosexual activity. They wanted an end to the ban against gays, lesbians and transgenders serving in the military. They wanted the right to gay marriage. They wanted the right to become foster parents and to adopt children. They wanted an end to employers rejecting homosexual job applicants. They wanted homosexual hate-crime laws passed, which punish people for the thoughts in their heads. They wanted therapy against homosexual impulses to be banned.

After achieving victory in many of its demands, the homosexual movement set its sights on newer, more radical milestones — such as getting rid of gender-identity birth certificates and driver licenses. They wanted people who refused to use preferred gender pronouns to be punished, fired or fined. They wanted bathrooms, showers and locker rooms in public schools to be gender neutral. They began pushing for transgenders to compete in biologically opposite-sex sports.

To appease transgenders, they wanted to redefine how people addressed parenthood and to change the language we use. Mothers should now be called "birthing people," they said, and breastfeeding became "chestfeeding."

As of the spring of 2022, several of these milestones have been reached and even put in the rear-view mirror.

Flush from their astounding victories in the late 20th and early 21st centuries, the LGBTQ movement has aggressive campaigns under way to force-feed homosexuality into homes, work, schools, television series, movies, churches, youth organizations, sports and even library events for toddlers.

A Rainbow of Rage

No longer is there a pretense that the rainbow flag represents tolerance, sexual diversity, acceptance, freedom of expression or inclusion. The LGBTQ rainbow flag has now been openly exposed as a banner of opposition, hatred, ill-will, malice, coercion, retaliation and, eventually, persecution against anyone opposed to the gay rights agenda.

A nation that only 50 years earlier saw homosexuality as a sin and a mental illness was being attacked on numerous fronts by powerful alliances trying to portray homosexuality as healthy, courageous, admirable and — in a way — even *elite*.

By as long ago as 2015, a vast chorus of media figures, academics, entertainers, politicians, judges and corporations had thrown their support behind the LGBTQ community. Their combined strength would put at risk the careers, reputations and fortunes of gay rights opponents.

Corporate giants, political leaders and uncompromising LGBTQ zealots sought to impose their unnatural and nonscientific views on society with determination and zeal. Their mantra became adherence, compulsion and obedience. They seemed not to care about lives destroyed or tarnished, businesses wrecked or religious and traditional institutions annihilated in the process.

Most notable has been the destruction of the largest scouting and youth organization in America: The 110-year-old Boy Scouts of America. In 2013, under pressure from the gay community and powerful corporations, the Boy Scouts of America shifted policy and lifted restrictions on sexual orientation for youth membership. Then, in 2015, the Boy Scouts of America would lift its ban on gay scout leaders.

Membership qualifications were changed despite tens of thousands of child sexual abuse cases against homosexual scoutmasters.

On February 18, 2020, the Boy Scouts of America filed for bankruptcy. The group was forced into a historic $850 million settlement to compensate 70,000 sexual abuse victims a year and a half later.

U.S. bankruptcy judge Laurie Silverstein would lament that the payoff had "the potential to end the Boy Scouts as it currently exists."

That's the destructive, poisonous potential of the LGBTQ community. They work their way into family-supporting, traditional-values organizations and religious ministries. They cloak themselves in a banner of fairness, inclusion and tolerance. Then they start to destroy those organizations from within.

The Tragedy of the Catholic Church

Comparable to legions of gay men creeping into the Boys Scouts of America over the decades, the Catholic Church had also long seen its ranks infiltrated by homosexual men who found roles — along with plenty of chances for clandestine sex with young people — as clergymen, youth leaders and advisers.

Alarm bells of homosexual child molestation cases in the Catholic Church began ringing in the late 1980s. It was during the same period that the LGBTQ sexual revolution was gaining momentum on the streets and taking hold of politically correct America's imagination.

French sociologist and journalist Frederic Martel spent four years interviewing 1,500 priests and found that an astounding 80 percent of Vatican priests were homosexual.

Martel made that shocking claim in a 540-page book called *In the closet of the Vatican.*

Martel, a confessed homosexual, was a former adviser to French Prime Minister Michel Rocard. Martel claimed priests didn't want to expose child sexual abuse in the Catholic Church for fear of exposing their own homosexuality.

As of 2019 nearly 1,700 homosexual priests in the U.S. were still active inside the Catholic Church ... many of them in close proximity to America's children.

According to the Associated Press, as of 2019 nearly 1,700 homosexual priests in the United States were still active inside the Catholic Church, serving as priests, deacons, teachers, coaches and counselors, many of them in close proximity to children.

Not only have homosexuals sunk the Catholic Church neck-deep into child sexual abuse lawsuits, they have cost the Church billions of dollars in settlements. As of 2018, the Church had paid nearly $4 billion to child sex abuse victims and their families.

By 2019, child sex abuse cases had forced 25 Catholic dioceses to either begin bankruptcy proceedings or declare bankruptcy.

In 2020, the Roman Catholic diocese of Harrisburg, Pennsylvania, filed for bankruptcy after it paid more than $12 million to 111 child victims whom clerics sexually abused.

Even after settlements with the 111 victims, the Harrisburg diocese nightmare was far from over. Two-hundred more sex abuse cases were still waiting in the wings to be resolved.

Having destroyed the Boy Scouts of America financially and crippled a large portion of the Catholic Church, largely through merely practicing their own preferred sexual activities, the homosexual activists have begun concentrating on the United Methodist Church, demanding to be ordained as clergy and leaders.

Those demands have the United Methodist Church teetering on the brink of division, internal revolt, loss of membership, and the destruction of its Book of Discipline and scriptural beliefs.

Targeting the Church and the Culture

Homosexuals want to infiltrate church ministries and denominations so they can destroy religious doctrine that opposes homosexual conduct, and they see it as a noble cause.

The LGBTQ community is obsessed and driven to feel accepted, get rid of feelings of guilt, and numb their God-given sense of shame. This is understandable. Few people want to wake up thinking they are on the wrong side of God.

Yet many homosexuals believe it's their mission to destroy institutions that consider their lifestyle a sin, a disease or a psychological illness — institutions that try to steer young people away from the sadness and danger of the gay lifestyle.

Their infiltration of the church to challenge time-honored religious doctrine, or even to redefine Jesus as gay himself, are attempts to sabotage religious objections to the gay lifestyle.

But even if the entire world accepted homosexuality as natural and normal (which it definitely does not), God Himself would not. Although they may try to create their own, gay version of the Jeffersonian Bible (from which Thomas Jefferson cut scripture that was inconvenient to his personal beliefs), they would never be able to ease God's sting of their conscience.

Romans chapter 2 verses 14-16 is clear:

"For when Gentiles who do not have the Law do instinctively the things of the Law, these, not having the Law, are a law to themselves, in that they show the work of the Law written in their hearts, their conscience bearing witness and their thoughts alternately accusing or else defending them, on the day when, according to my gospel, God will judge the secrets of men through Christ Jesus."

That's precisely the type of scripture the gay and lesbian community would like to see expunged from the Bible.

By 2010, the organized LGBTQ community was at war with those who frowned upon homosexual conduct or refused to accept homosexuality as a legitimate, healthy and normal lifestyle.

A massive media campaign was launched to shame, ostracize and minimize — even humiliate — anyone who objected to homosexual sex or the gay rights agenda.

Leaders of the LGBTQ movement would label opponents as homophobes, hate-mongers, religious bigots, even Nazis.

Although frequently used to bring about social change, name calling has historically failed as a tool to modify behavior. The homosexual community itself is a case in point. Before the 20th century, homosexuals lived with such slurs as fag, dyke, pansy and far worse. Those insults did not prevent gays and lesbians from forming a robust community of activists, educators, entertainers, politicians, authors and business leaders.

Having failed at name calling, homosexual activists developed a strategy they hoped would finally shame their opponents into obedience and reluctant acceptance:

They got into Hollywood.

Television and film scripts were purposefully written to disparage opponents of homosexuality by making them into brainless, bigoted characters

Hollywood is fully on board with the gay pride movement, and frequently disparages Chrstians, and anyone who oposes the gay agenda, in film and TV.* (Flickr photo by Minnemom)

deserving vicious humiliation. Typically, the stories end with the bigot brought nearly to tears in shameful repentance — or in some cases acknowledging that he or she is, in fact, homosexual but unable to accept it.

Over the years, the constant drumbeat of public humiliation toward gay rights opponents — presented in movies, television shows, theater and song — did help to silence detractors. Still, that strategy would never secure what the gay and lesbian community desired most: Acceptance, love, hero status and admiration.

After all, they were a PRIDE movement deserving to be treated like superstars.

The Pride Offensive

To this end, the homosexual community launched a national media campaign to convince the American public that the word Pride was synonymous with being gay.

The moniker "gay pride" originated in the 1964 novel *Last Exit to Brooklyn*, in which author Hubert Shelby created a homosexual character who "took pride in being a homosexual by feeling intellectually and esthetically superior to those who weren't gay."

A recurring theme among gay Pride proponents is they are somehow more intelligent, sensitive, artistic and beautiful than non-gays.

In 2012, *The Journal of Biosocial Science* reported that "gay people are typically born with more intelligence than the average heterosexual." And that "smart people [are] more willing to engage with same-sex desires."

> ❝ **Gay people are typically born with more intelligence than the average heterosexual.**

The journal also made the astounding claim that the more sex partners homosexuals have, the "brighter" they tend to be.

According to Dr. Satoshi Kanazawa, lead author of the study, homosexual men were "very bright" if they averaged 2.4 sex partners, while straight men and monogamous homosexuals were deemed "very dull."

Homosexuals want to feel intellectually and morally superior to people they see as "judging" their lifestyle. Simply shaming an opponent is not enough. Their "Pride" needs to be seen, trumpeted, showcased, paraded and shoved into the faces of anyone who might disapprove of it.

They need to be visible *everywhere* — in commercials, movies, television shows, ads, police forces, churches, the business world, schools and colleges, clubs, theme parks, governments, social influencers, sports, teachers, fashion and publishing.

An Affinity for Young Children

For at least the past two decades, homosexuality promoters have been openly targeting children through what they watch, listen to, learn and even eat. Children learn about homosexuality in sex education classes. They study controversial homosexual figures during history lessons. Children's products and snacks are branded with homosexual symbols. Beloved cartoon shows have introduced same-sex characters, including children with two moms or two dads. Superheroes have been refashioned into LGBTQ champions. Gay pride flags and posters now decorate the halls and classrooms of many public schools. School libraries have stocked their shelves with novels and fairytales about the gay, lesbian and transgender lifestyles.

Yet despite these aggressive efforts to target the young, America's youth have grown increasingly resistant to homosexual indoctrination. Not only are they rejecting homosexual behavior, but they are becoming less accepting of homosexual family members, teachers, doctors and homosexuality-promoting sex-education classes.

The massive propaganda campaign to get America's youth to accept homosexuality as an alternative lifestyle is, in fact, failing miserably. The largest segment of America's population growing more resistant to embracing homosexuality is actually young adults between the ages of 18 and 34.

From 2016 to 2018, a national pro-gay lobby group called GLAAD (Gay and Lesbian Alliance Against Defamation) commissioned a Harris Poll to survey youth acceptance of homosexuality. What they learned was shocking, at least to them.

In 2016, 63 percent of 18- to 34-year-olds said they felt comfortable interacting with gays and lesbians. But by 2017, that number had dropped 10 percent to just 53 percent who felt at ease around homosexuals. A year later, those numbers would fall even further. In 2018, only 45 percent said they felt comfortable around gays and lesbians — a drop of 18 percent in just two years.

That was not the only negative news in the Harris poll for the LGBTQ community. Even as it learned that a clear 55 percent majority of young Americans felt uncomfortable interacting with homosexuals, it also discovered that young adults were feeling increasingly uncomfortable with family members coming out as gay or lesbian. Those numbers jumped from 24 percent opposed to gay family members in 2016 to 34 percent in 2018.

Neither are young Americans growing more accepting of gay and lesbian teachers. In 2016, only 24 percent opposed homosexual instructors. By 2018, that number had risen to 34 percent.

And whereas in 2016, only 27 percent of young Americans were opposed to sex education classes in the public schools, that number rose by 12 percent — reaching 39 percent in 2018.

The polling results have become so deflating for the gay and lesbian community — with numbers that highlighted the growing resentment among young people at having homosexuality crammed into everything they see, eat, learn or watch — that GLAAD has stopped releasing results of the annual survey.

But that's not how the LGBTQ movement would analyze its failure. Instead, they lay the blame exclusively at the feet of Bible-believing Christians who preach that homosexuality is a sin.

They see themselves in a vicious tug-of-war. On one end of the rope are churches, religious ministries and evangelical leaders who use the Bible to condemn homosexuality as abnormal, against God's laws, and self-destructive. On the opposite end of the rope are gay rights advocates who use massive marketing campaigns to promote homosexuality as glamorous, trendy, natural and healthy.

To win this tug-of-war and not to be pulled into their own pool of muck, the LGBTQ community decided to go nuclear against Bible-believing Christians and churches. They believe Christians who fail to kneel at the altar of gay acceptance should be silenced with hefty fines, loss of jobs, compulsory sensitivity training courses, crippling lawsuits and even jail.

Setting the stage for these draconian measures were homosexual propaganda machines that depicted Christian adversaries as dangerous hatemongers. Eager to help, and already on the battlefield, was the controversial and fabulously wealthy "human rights organization," the Southern Poverty Law Center (SPLC).

Formed in 1971, the SPLC of Montgomery, Alabama, initially focused on racial discrimination and death penalty issues. By 1979 the SPLC had shot to national fame with a constant bombardment of lawsuits against the Ku Klux Klan. Its frequent favorable verdicts would eventually force the KKK into bankruptcy, with the SPLC seizing its assets.

In a 1998 case alone, the SPLC won a verdict of $37.8 million against the KKK on behalf of the 100-year-old Macedonia Baptist Church, a black place of worship in Manning, S.C.

The SPLC legal campaign against the KKK was so successful it would later launch a project called KlanWatch to monitor the activities of the Ku Klux Klan. In 2007, the project's name was changed to HateWatch so it could include "anti-LGBTQ hate" groups and possibly rake in even more donations.

The SPLC writes that most entries on their "anti-LGBTQ hate" list are "groups (that) primarily consist of Christian Right groups ..."

A "Christian Right group," the SPLC explains, is an organization that uses "God's name" when opposing homosexuality, same-sex marriage, gay adoption or a myriad of other social-activist issues put forth by the LGBT community.

The definition makes any church or religious organization that believes in the fundamentals of the Bible into a hate group.

The SPLC boasts that its goal is to drive these religious-based organizations to ruin by crippling their donation sources, burying them in lawsuits, depriving them of public forums (such as media interviews and speaking engagements), and destroying their reputations.

Each year the SPLC issues disparaging press releases about these religious organizations, listing their locations and names, with little detail regarding their alleged hate activity. Each year media outlets obediently pick up the "news," publishing the names despite lacking any credible evidence of the alleged acts of hate.

Some have accused the Southern Poverty Law Center of being a hate group itself for the way it dangerously aggravates hatred.

Such was the case on Aug. 15, 2012, when Floyd Lee Corkins II walked into the lobby of the Family Research Council's headquarters in Washington, D.C., carrying a 9mm pistol, two magazines and 50 rounds of ammunition.

Although the Southern Poverty Law Center claims to stand for "fighting hate, teaching tolerance, and seeking justice," it has no tolerance for Christian groups, conservatives, or anyone who opposes the homosexual agenda.* (Flickr photo by Ian Abbott, SPLC)

At the time — and still today — the Family Research Council was listed as a hate group by the SPLC. On its public website, the SPLC accused the organization of having an agenda "to denigrate LBGTQ people" because they opposed "same-sex marriage, hate crime laws, anti-bullying programs and (supported) the repeal of the military's Don't Ask, Don't Tell policy and gays serving in the military."

Reading those comments, Floyd Lee Corkins told police it made him want to kill everyone inside the family-values organization.

Before entering FRC headquarters, Corkins first stopped at a Chik-Fil-A restaurant to buy 15 filet sandwiches, which he intended to rub in the faces of dead employees after he killed them. Chik-Fil-A, a highly successful restaurant chain, has outspoken Christian management and policies.

However, upon entering the building, Corkins was met by an unarmed security guard, 46-year-old Leonardo Johnson. Corkins immediately shot the security guard, wounding him in the arm. With the help of a few others, the brave but wounded guard tackled Corkins and held him to the ground until police arrived to arrest him.

In 2013, a judge sentenced Corkins to 25 years in prison.

The SPLC named 65 anti-gay groups in its 2020 reporting, identifying them by name and location.

God-fearing organizations and leaders know their names are on that list primarily to make them the targets of pro-homosexual activists. The targeting doesn't have to involve physical violence. That's still a rarity, thank God. But people and groups have been targeted for other forms of sabotage. Their websites have been hacked, their bank accounts shut down, their media appearances canceled. Their credit card accounts have been closed. Their books have been removed from online bookstores such as Amazon. Their educational videos have been censored or deleted from YouTube. Their social media accounts have been suppressed, suspended or closed.

It's a calculated strategy not only to silence well-known religious figures but to induce a chilling effect that silences parents, business executives, workers, government employees, entertainers, sports figures, educators ... anyone big or small who dares stand in the way of the homosexual agenda.

This strategy has recently acquired its own unique name: It's known as "Cancel Culture."

Putting Straightjackets on the Straight

Incidents of Christians being "canceled" — that is, bullied, threatened and compelled to comply with the homosexual agenda at the risk of their livelihoods — are too plentiful to fully recount here. They range from the subtle to the outrageous. Some make headlines, but most are simply ignored by the mainstream media.

These incidents consist mainly of people being fired from their jobs, fined, jailed, ordered into group-think "sensitivity training"

25

classes, or run out of business for offending the tender sensibilities of the LGBTQ community.

We'll talk about a few.

In Bloomsburg, Pennsylvania , a bridal shop was forced to close in 2018 after the owner family received death threats to themselves and their children for refusing to outfit a lesbian wedding. W.W. Bridal Boutique said angry homosexuals left messages on its company phones that they would burn down their building, shoot the proprietors in the head and even rape their children. Fearing for their safety, sadly, the owners shut their doors.

In Morehead, Kentucky, in 2015, county clerk Kim Davis was ordered to report to jail after she refused to issue a marriage license to two homosexual men. Her jail sentence in that small town of less than 8,000 became national and international news.

Davis argued that as a conscientious Christian, issuing a marriage license to a same-sex couple would be a violation of her religious faith. To put her signature on the license, she felt, would be to implicitly endorse homosexual marriage. Her refusal came on the heels of a 2015 Supreme Court ruling that legalized gay marriage just months earlier in the 2015 Obergefell v. Hodges case.

When Davis ignored a court order to issue the license, she was charged with contempt by Judge David Bunning. He remanded her to jail until she agreed to issue the license to gay lovers David Ermold and David Moore. She was released after only five days via a compromise that required her to "not interfere in any way ... with efforts of her deputy clerks to issue marriage licenses to all legally eligible couples."

Her jailing led former governor of Arkansas and presidential candidate Mike Huckabee to say, "I think it's fair to say that Christian convictions are under attack as never before. Not just in our lifetime, but ever before in the history of this great nation. We are moving rapidly toward the criminalization of Christianity."

Davis was later sued by four gay couples over her refusal to issue them marriage licenses. A court awarded the couples $224,000 in 2017. Davis appealed the decision to the United States Supreme Court, but lost in a unanimous decision.

Justice Clarence Thomas did, however, issue this serious warning in his opinion:

> *"Davis may have been one of the first victims of this Court's cavalier treatment of religion in its Obergefell decision, but she will not*

be the last. Due to Obergefell, those with sincerely held religious beliefs concerning marriage will find it increasingly difficult to participate in society without running afoul of Obergefell and its effect on other anti-discrimination laws."

Topping the list in terms of both publicity and unrelenting homosexual activist attacks is the case of baker Jack Phillips, who founded Masterpiece Cakeshop in Lakewood, Colorado.

Phillips opened his family-owned bakery in 1993. In July 2012 two homosexual men, Charlie Craig and David Mullins, entered the business and requested a gay-themed wedding cake. Phillips politely declined, saying it would be a violation of his religious faith to design such a cake.

The couple immediately filed a complaint with the Colorado Civil Rights Commission for sexual orientation discrimination. The commission, taking the side of the gay men, ordered Phillips to either start designing cakes celebrating homosexual ceremonies or stop offering cakes to all wedding customers — a service that comprised 40 percent of his business. Phillips was also ordered to "rehabilitate" his staff in regards to serving same-sex couples.

"My 87-year-old mom works here," Phillips told FOX News. "And she says she's not being rehabilitated ... Obey Christ rather than worry about what man can do to you."

Coming to the rescue of Masterpiece Cakeshop was Alliance Defending Freedom. Attorney Nicolle Martin promised that the nonprofit religious liberty group would "continue to stand with Jack against overreach and tyranny by the state."

That is what they did, all the way to the United States Supreme Court, which granted Phillips a stunning victory in June 2018. In a 7-2 decision, justices ruled that the Colorado civil rights commission showed "clear and impermissible hostility toward (Phillips') sincere religious beliefs."

The attacks against Phillips and his cakeshop did not end there, of course.

In June 2017, a transgender attorney, Autumn Scardina, called the business to request a gender-transition (male to female) birthday cake, one that was pink on the inside and blue on the outside. Once again Phillips refused.

"Phillips declined to create the cake with the blue-and-pink design because it would have celebrated messages contrary to his religious belief that sex — the status of being male or female — is given by God, is biologically determined, is not determined by perceptions or feelings, and cannot be chosen or changed," his attorney said.

On June 28, 2018, the Colorado Civil Rights Commission ruled that there was "probable cause" that Phillips discriminated against Scardina based on "her" gender identity.

Aubrey Elenis, the director of the civil rights division, said Phillips had "denied her equal enjoyment of a place of public accommodation."

On June 15, 2021 a Denver judge sided with the Colorado

Christian-owned businesses, which decline to provide provide gay-themed products or services for gay weddings have been sued in recent years.* (Flickr photo by Dominique Cappronnier)

commission and ordered Phillips to pay the transgender attorney $500. Alliance Defending Freedom is appealing the case as of this writing.

"Jack has been harassed for nearly a decade for living by his faith and making artistic decisions that artists have always made," ADF attorney Jake Warner explained. "That's why we have appealed this decision and will continue to defend the freedom of all Americans to peacefully live and work according to their core convictions without fear of government punishment."

To detail each and every attack, plot and attempted sabotage of a Christian business, organization or individual by homosexual activists would require its own book. But here are a few more:

In Charlotte, Mich., farmers Steven and Bridget Tennes inflamed the wrath of city officials after they declared their wedding venue would not host gay weddings. For years children visiting 213-acre Country Mills Farms have enjoyed picking their own apples, blueberries, peaches, sunflowers and pumpkins. But despite the farm's wholesome and beloved reputation, the City of East Lansing retaliated against the 50-year-old establishment by forbidding the owners to sell produce at the East Lansing market.

In Virginia, two teachers were fired after refusing to address transgender students with inaccurate, contrived pronouns. Physical education teacher Tanner Cross was fired in 2021 after he told a school board he would not refer to a biological boy as "she" or her," or vice-versa. "It's lying to a child. It's abuse to a child, and it's sinning against our God," he said.

Virginia French-language teacher Peter Vlaming was also fired when he "misgendered" a transsexual student at West Point High School.

"I explained to my principal that I couldn't in good conscience pronounce masculine pronouns to refer to a girl," Vlaming told *The Daily Signal* in an interview. "He gave me an official written reprimand that said it was the first step in a process that would lead to my termination." Just before Christmas of 2018, the school board voted unanimously to fire Vlaming.

In Atlanta, fire chief Kelvin Cochran was fired in 2014 after writing a Bible-study book called, *Who Told You That You Were Naked?* The book described those having gay sex, or sex outside of marriage, as wicked. U.S. District Judge Leigh Martin May upheld his firing, saying it was "not unreasonable for the city to fear" his views might cause "public erosion of trust in the fire department."

Presumably, according to this judge's opinion, this Bible-believing fire chief might allow a home to burn to the ground if it was inhabited by a homosexual or a couple engaged in extra-marital sex.

As a final example, in 2021 the Atlanta City Council told all city workers they must take a course in "LGBTQ cultural humility training" if they wanted to keep their jobs.

Of course it is not just adults the LGBTQ movement is trying to punish and rein in. Children may even be their preferred targets.

In one outrageous July, 2021, incident, the San Francisco Gay Men's Chorus performed and posted on the Internet a song called: *We're Coming for your Children.*

"We'll convert your children, reaching one and all," the song taunts. "We're coming for them. We're coming for your children ... All their brothers and sisters ... Your kids will start converting you!"

In August of the same year, shortly after the song's publication, California high school teacher Kristin Pitzen took the words to heart. Pitzen posted a video of herself bragging that she tricked her students in the Newport Mesa School District into saying the Pledge of Allegiance to the gay, LGBTQ rainbow flag. After removing the American flag from her classroom (she said the flag made her feel "uncomfortable"), a student asked exactly where he should now say the pledge.

"We do have a flag in the class that you can pledge your allegiance to," she told him. Laughing in her selfie video, she says: "And he goes: 'Oh, that one?'" as she points to the gay flag hanging in her classroom.

In a previous video, and while wearing rainbow glasses, earrings and suspenders, Pitzen had said, "I pledge allegiance to the queers." She was later fired.

In Florida, also in 2021, a teacher took her kids from Wilton Manors Elementary on a field trip to visit a local bar. A field trip for little kids to any bar would have been alarming enough, but this was a well-known, local homosexual hangout in Broward County. School board member Sarah Leonardi actually praised the hare-brained decision to expose little children to the gay bar lifestyle, saying she was "proud" the kids were "connecting with the vibrant small businesses in my district."

> ❛ **We do have a flag in the class that you can pledge your allegiance to ... I pledge allegiance to the queers.**

The targeting and sexual grooming of children by the LGBTQ "community" became national news again in the fall of 2021 when parents across the nation discovered a book called *Gender Queer* in many public-school libraries. The book, true to parents' complaints, contains graphic depictions of gay sex, pictures of sex toys and abundant obscene language and illustrations.

When a parent in Florida, Jacob Engels, tried reading a passage from the book during an Orange County school board meeting, he was removed from the building for using "vulgar language." The passage he recited graphically described the use of sex toys.

"Mr. Engels, you're out of order. Remove him from the chambers," ordered Board Chair Teresa Jacobs.

These incidents do more than any argument to make the point of this booklet.

The success of the LGBTQ movement is built on fear, intimidation, secrecy, bullying and threats. From the viewpoint of the gay rights movement, this strategy is working very well.

Laws are being changed. Opponents are being punished for biblical, biological and scientific views on sex and gender. The careers of detractors are being crushed. Businesses and individuals are being driven into bankruptcy. Some face debilitating lawsuits; many more have become social pariahs. Court victories for LGBT are now easy and even predictable. The media, academia, Hollywood and political leaders have jointly used their bully pulpits to preach and champion the gay rights agenda.

Perhaps most notable is that homosexuality seems to be celebrated in any place where content is edited, regulated or curated: television shows, amusement parks, museums, government flagpoles, street murals, schools, candy bar labels, church signs, liquor bottles, and even as decorations for baby carriages.

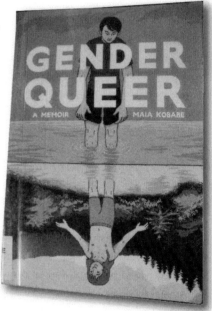

When a parent tried to read a passage from the school book Gender Queer, he was removed from the building for using "vulgar language."* (Flickr photo by Earthworm)

In 1978, the gay community stole God's rainbow and turned it into a weapon to twist the American people's hearts, souls and minds and then bully them into accepting the homosexual lifestyle as normal.

Looking for the End of the Rainbow

But there's always a price to pay when you steal from God, no matter how clever and successful your crime might seem.

Witness the tragic biblical story of the Philistines capturing the Ark of the Covenant after their victory over the Israelites in a battle near Ebenezer (1 Samuel 4).

Israel's high priest Eli fell off his chair upon learning of the Ark's capture. He broke his neck and died. The rest of the Jewish nation mourned in horror.

Upon learning of Eli's death, the death of her husband and brother-in-law and the capture of the Ark, Eli's daughter-in-law, Phinehas, died while giving birth to her son. A woman helping Phinehas during that delivery named the surviving child Ichabod, saying,

"The glory has departed from Israel!"

In much the same way, the LGBT movement's seizure of God's rainbow both stole and ransacked its glory from His people.

Bear in mind, however, that the Philistines' capture of the ark came with a heavy price that was not inflicted on them by man, but by God.

While in possession of the Philistines in Ashdod the ark toppled and dismembered their idol, Dagon, leaving nothing but a stump. Then the hand of God took vengeance on the people of Ashdod and "made them feel devastated and struck them with tumors."

The ark was then moved to Goth, where the people fared no better.

" ... the hand of the Lord was against the city, creating a very great panic; and He struck the people of the city, from the young to the old, so that tumors broke out on them."

So the ark was then sent to Ekron, where the villagers were none too pleased to see its arrival.

"They have brought the ark of the God of Israel to us, to kill us and our people!"

The city was in a panic — a "deadly panic" as the Bible tells us. Many died, and those who did not die were struck with tumors.

The Philistines finally came to their senses and decided to send the ark back to Israel.

It is hard to overlook the parallel between the wretched, physical sufferings of the Philistines after they commandeered God's ark and those of the disease-ridden gay community after they stole God's rainbow.

Name a sexually transmitted disease and it is a strong presence in the highly promiscuous LGBQ community: gonorrhea, syphilis, anal warts, herpes, monkeypox.

The CDC even admitted in 2015: "While anyone can become infected with an STD, young people and gay and bisexual men are at greatest risk."

- In the case of syphilis, the CDC states, "Men who have sex with men account for 83 percent of male cases where the sex of the sex partner is known."

- Not surprisingly, homosexual men account for 81 percent of HIV diagnoses.

- Gay men (relative to straight men) rank highest in hepatitis, depression, anxiety, prostate and colon cancer, alcoholism and suicide.

- According to the National Institute on Drug Abuse, "Surveys thus far have found that sexual minorities (LGBTQ) have higher rates of substance misuse and substance use disorders (SUDs) than people who identify as heterosexual."

Beyond illnesses, life-threatening diseases and medical hardships (insurance costs, loss of jobs, medical expenses), LGBT-identifying people suffer from an overall low quality of life.

While gay festivals and publicity may portray a life of "pride" and joy, the community is also known for loneliness, homelessness, bitter anger and isolation.

Writing for The Huffington Post, gay-activist Michael Hobbes made these observations:

- Gay people are up to 10 times more likely to commit suicide.
- Twice as likely to suffer major depressive episodes.
- Three-quarters of New York City gay men abuse drugs or alcohol.

And then this:

"Despite all the talk of our 'chosen families,' gay men have fewer close friends than straight people or gay women. In a survey of care-providers at HIV clinics, one respondent told researchers: 'It's not a question of them not knowing how to save their lives. It's a question of them knowing if their lives are worth saving.'"

No one can state definitively that these scourges are in fact God's retribution on the LGBT community for stealing His rainbow.

The Bible, however, is surprisingly clear:

"Do not be deceived, God is not mocked; for whatever a man sows, this he will also reap. For the one who sows to his own flesh will from the flesh reap corruption, but the one who sows to the Spirit will from the Spirit reap eternal life."

(Galations 6:7-8)

---

* Flickr photos are used in this publication under the Creative Commons license, which can be accessed at this web site:

https://creativecommons.org/licenses/by-nc-sa/2.0/legalcode

Made in the USA
Columbia, SC
13 September 2022

66749885R00020